Table of Contents

Introduction 1

I. Food Safety Working Group Initiatives and Accomplishments 4
    A. Prevention of Foodborne Illness 4
        1. Reduce Bacterial Pathogens in Foods 4
        2. Improved Produce Safety 6
        3. Preventing Intentional Adulteration 8
        4. Other Preventive Measures in Food Safety 8
    B. Enhanced Food Safety Surveillance and Compliance 9
        1. Disease surveillance 9
        2. Reportable Food Registry 10
        3. Antimicrobial Resistance 11
        4. Import Safety 11
    C. Food Safety Response 14
        1. Strengthening the National Traceback and Response System 14
        2. Recalls 16
    D. Additional Agency Coordination and Capacity Building 17
    E. Retail Food Safety 18
    F. Consumer Education 19

II. Food Safety Working Group 2011-12 Agenda and Beyond 21
    A. Greater Prevention 21
        1. Pre-Harvest Food Safety 21
        2. Upcoming Preventive Control Standards 22
        3. Retail Food Safety 23
    B. Enhanced Surveillance and Compliance 23
        1. Domestic Inspection and Compliance 23
        2. Import Safety 24
        3. Foodborne Illness Surveillance and Incident Investigation 24

    4. Product Tracing 25

C. Improved Response 26

    1. Outbreak Response 26

    2. Data Analysis 27

D. Consumer Education 27

E. Partnerships 28

Introduction

American consumers deserve to trust the safety of the food they purchase for themselves and their families. While we enjoy one of the safest food supplies in the world, it requires constant monitoring. We need to be able to rapidly identify and address risks to our food supply as a result of new disease agents, new food technologies, changes in U.S. demographic and dietary patterns, and an abundance of food imports resulting from an increasingly globalized food supply. In recent years, consumers and industry alike have been impacted by illnesses associated with food products, such as ground beef, peppers, peanut butter, spinach, shell eggs, and cookie dough, among others. While regulatory and industry efforts have over time improved food safety considerably, the Centers for Disease Control and Prevention has recently estimated that 1 in 6 Americans suffers from foodborne illness annually, resulting in 128,000 hospitalizations and 3,000 deaths per year, most of which are preventable.

The public health consequences of foodborne illness remain significant. The impact reaches well beyond the number of cases. Foodborne illnesses result in billions of dollars in medical costs, as well as significant economic losses to the food industry when illness outbreaks and contamination incidents undermine consumer confidence in affected commodities, require large recalls, and diminish demand. American consumers have high expectations for the safety of the food supply. While all risks will never be eliminated, the public rightfully expects that the government and the food industry do everything that can reasonably be done to prevent food safety problems.

> The Food Safety Working Group's core mission is to strengthen federal efforts and develop strategies to improve food safety.

The federal government has taken important steps to protect an increasingly complex food supply. In March 2009, President Obama created the Food Safety Working Group (FSWG), a central coordinating mechanism for the federal government's food safety activities that is led by the Department of Health and Human Services (HHS) and the U.S. Department of Agriculture (USDA). The FSWG's core mission is to strengthen federal efforts and develop short-term and long-term strategies to improve food safety. Partner agencies include HHS's Food and Drug Administration (FDA), USDA's Food Safety and Inspection Service (FSIS), and HHS's Centers for Disease Control and Prevention (CDC), as well as the Environmental Protection Agency (EPA), Department of Homeland Security, Department of Commerce, Department of State, and the Office of the United States Trade Representative. The White House Domestic Policy Council convenes the FSWG.

The premise underlying the FSWG's creation is that coordination among federal agencies is essential to protect consumers in our highly diverse, global food system. Coordination and cooperation are necessary through every stage of the production and consumption process—"from farm to table." FSWG member departments and agencies thus share information and experience about all aspects of food safety. Such coordination strengthens the scientific and technical infrastructure to support a modern food safety system.

Collaboration with state, local and foreign governments as well as partnership with the private sector is likewise crucial.

The FSWG recognizes that through enhanced collaboration and selective, risk-based deployment of government efforts, the federal agencies can best utilize all available food safety resources to ensure the effectiveness and efficiency of the food safety system and improve food safety programs.

By clarifying responsibilities and improving accountability, the FSWG has already strengthened the nation's food safety system. The FDA has created a new position, Deputy Commissioner for Foods, who is empowered to restructure and revitalize FDA's work developing a new food safety system.

The FSWG agencies have also taken substantial steps to modernize federal food safety. For instance, FSIS launched the Public Health Information System (PHIS), a comprehensive data analytics system to better detect and respond to foodborne hazards. FDA has increased the number of domestic and foreign risk-based inspections it undertakes and is pursuing a comprehensive, farm-to-table strategy for preventing food safety problems.

> **Three-Dimensional Approach:**
> 1. Prevention
> 2. Surveillance
> 3. Response

CDC has begun development of next-generation laboratory methods and new epidemiological tools for investigating multi-state outbreaks in partnership with State, local, tribal, and territorial health departments.

The following pages detail some of the FSWG's other core efforts and accomplishments over the past two years to strengthen the food safety system through greater prevention, surveillance, and response.

In July 2009, the FSWG submitted a Report of Key Findings to the President. That report emphasized a three-dimensional approach to enhancing public health through greater food safety:

- **"Prevention"**—establish science-based best practices to reduce the risk of illness among entities that produce, process, and distribute food;

- **"Surveillance"**—the ongoing, systematic collection and analysis of containment, public health, and molecular data, throughout the farm-to-fork continuum, for use in preventing and controlling foodborne illnesses; and

- **"Response"**—rapidly detect and terminate foodborne illness outbreaks and contamination when and where they do occur.

Over the past two years, these aims have provided the organizing framework for the FSWG's efforts, and they will continue to do so going forward.

Two years after its creation, the time is right to assess the FSWG's efforts to date and to anticipate its agenda over the next two years. Accordingly, this Progress Report summarizes some of the FSWG's accomplishments to improve prevention, surveillance, and response. It also identifies some of the FSWG's priorities over the next year and beyond, including activities necessary to implement the FDA Food Safety Modernization Act (FSMA), which was signed into law on January 4, 2011.

> The bi-partisan passage of FSMA was one of the most significant accomplishments in the history of food safety in the United States.

The passage of FSMA is one of the most significant accomplishments in the history of food safety in the United States. It was passed on a bi-partisan basis with support from a broad coalition of industry, consumer and public health groups and is grounded in the same principles that the FSWG embraced in its 2009 report.

FSMA calls on FDA, working in partnership with other federal, state and local agencies and the food industry, to build a modern new system of food safety oversight that harnesses the best available practices to prevent food safety problems. FSMA also calls on CDC to strengthen public health surveillance and response networks in partnership with state and local health departments. Implementation of FSMA will be a major FSWG priority in the years ahead.

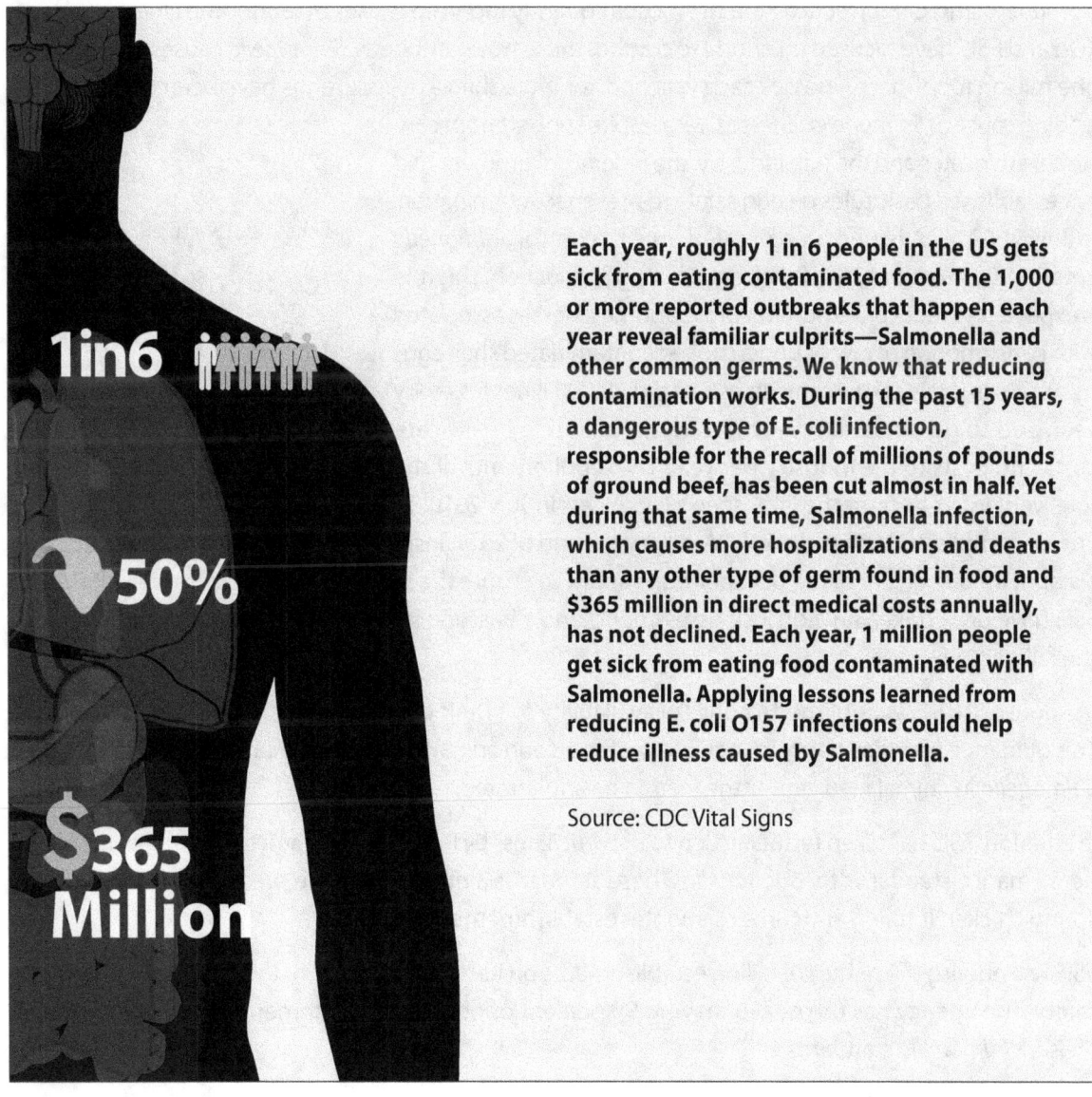

Each year, roughly 1 in 6 people in the US gets sick from eating contaminated food. The 1,000 or more reported outbreaks that happen each year reveal familiar culprits—Salmonella and other common germs. We know that reducing contamination works. During the past 15 years, a dangerous type of E. coli infection, responsible for the recall of millions of pounds of ground beef, has been cut almost in half. Yet during that same time, Salmonella infection, which causes more hospitalizations and deaths than any other type of germ found in food and $365 million in direct medical costs annually, has not declined. Each year, 1 million people get sick from eating food contaminated with Salmonella. Applying lessons learned from reducing E. coli O157 infections could help reduce illness caused by Salmonella.

Source: CDC Vital Signs

I. Food Safety Working Group Initiatives and Accomplishments

A. Prevention of Foodborne Illness

Prevention is the front line of food safety defense. The FSWG agencies have taken substantial steps to reduce the occurrence of foodborne illness by preventing the contamination and adulteration of foods. They have focused on *Salmonella, E. coli, Campylobacter,* and *Listeria* among other causes of foodborne illness.

1. Reduce Bacterial Pathogens in Foods

Salmonella and *Campylobacter* are the most frequently reported causes of foodborne illness, and both FDA and FSIS have focused on efforts to combat these two pathogens. *Salmonella* causes an estimated one million foodborne illnesses each year and, for more than a decade, eggs have been identified as a leading cause of *Salmonella* illnesses. Yet, despite support from consumer advocates and the egg industry, the federal government had not established basic rules on egg safety to prevent contamination. In July 2009, FDA issued an egg safety rule to control *Salmonella* Enteritidis contamination of shell eggs during production. This rule is expected to reduce the number of foodborne illnesses associated with consumption of raw or undercooked contaminated shell eggs by approximately 60 percent, an estimated 79,000 illnesses every year, and to generate savings of nearly $1 billion in healthcare costs and costs to the industry per year. The requirements of the rule went into effect for the largest egg producers in July 2010. To ensure compliance with the rule, FDA will, by the end of 2011, inspect 600 of the largest producers, who account for 80 percent of the U.S. shell egg supply. To ensure the safety of liquid eggs as well, USDA and FSIS have undertaken an "Egg Risk Assessment," and a baseline study on liquid egg products began in the fall of 2011.

> FDA's egg safety rule sets new requirements that will prevent 79,000 illnesses and save $1 billion each year.

In August 2010, FDA published a notice of availability of a Draft Guidance for Salmonella in Animal Feed. This guidance provides clarity to regulatory officials and animal feed industry on when the presence of *Salmonella* in animal feed causes the feed to be adulterated.

In addition, FSIS has taken further action to prevent illness by implementing stricter pathogen reduction performance standards for *Salmonella*. These standards aim to reduce the presence of *Salmonella* in young chicken (broiler) and turkey slaughter establishments.

FSIS will publish the names of failing establishments on its website to inform the public of risks to food safety. The agency has the goal of having 90 percent of poultry establishments meet or exceed the revised *Salmonella* standards.

FSIS also implemented its first-ever pathogen reduction performance standards for *Campylobacter* in poultry establishments. Revising current performance standards—and setting new ones—will continue the reduction of pathogens and result in safer products.

> FSIS implemented its first-ever pathogen reduction standards for root causes of high-frequency foodborne illnesses in poultry establishments.

In addition, FSIS announced that it will expand the Salmonella Initiative Program (SIP) to help reduce *Salmonella* in raw meat and poultry products, a program that aims to reduce and eliminate pathogens before products reach consumers. This voluntary, incentive-based program will allow participating establishments to operate under certain regulatory waivers in order to try new procedures, equipment or processing techniques to better control *Salmonella*. Establishments under SIP will collect product samples, use these samples to test for common foodborne pathogens such as *Salmonella, Campylobacter* and *E. coli,* and share this internal food safety data with FSIS. This approach improves food safety by encouraging industry to test for and take action to reduce pathogens.

E. coli O157:H7. The bacterial strain *E. coli* O157:H7 causes diarrhea, abdominal pain, and fever in approximately 63,000 Americans each year following consumption of contaminated food. In an estimated one in fifteen patients, a serious complication known as "Hemolytic-Uremic Syndrome" develops. Patients with this complication can suffer intense pain, anemia, kidney failure, and even death. In recent years, this bacterium has caused outbreaks associated with meat and spinach, among other foods. In March 2010, FSIS reissued a directive and began a new verification testing program for beef bench trim (a key cut of meat used in making ground beef) and for establishments that handle beef, to ensure they are taking action to reduce the presence of *E. coli* O157:H7. The directive includes instructions to both domestic and important inspection personnel for sampling raw beef products for FSIS verification testing for *E. coli* O157:H7. In addition, it outlines actions that FSIS will take if samples of raw ground beef, raw ground beef components, or raw beef patty components test positive for *E. coli* O157:H7. Finally, it includes instructions for other verification activities concerning *E. coli* O157:H7. FSIS has also increased their sampling to find this pathogen, focusing largely on the components that go into making ground beef. Foodborne Diseases Active Surveillance Network's ("FoodNet") 2010 data indicates that the substantial decrease in incidence of reported *E. coli* O157:H7 infections met the national Healthy People objective for 2010, and a further decrease of 50% is called for to meet the 2020 national objective.

> Foodborne Diseases Active Surveillance Network's ("FoodNet") 2010 data indicates that the substantial decrease in incidence of reported *E. coli* O157:H7 infections met the national Healthy People objective for 2010, and a further decrease of 50% is called for to meet the 2020 national objective.

E. coli Non-O157. FSIS announced that six additional serogroups of pathogenic *E. coli* will be declared adulterants in non-intact raw beef—raw ground beef, its components, and tenderized steaks. These products will be prohibited from sale to consumers, and FSIS is launching a testing program to detect these dangerous pathogens and prevent them from reaching consumers. CDC estimates that over 112,000 foodborne illnesses occur every year from non-O157 STEC and that the six new *E. coli* serogroups (O26, O103, O45, O111, O121 and O145) are responsible for the greatest number of non-O157 Shiga toxin-producing *E. coli* (STEC) illnesses, hospitalizations and deaths in the U.S. *E. coli* O157:H7 already is an adulterant in these products.

> FSIS declared 6 additional types of *E. coli* as adulterants, prohibiting their sale to consumers in raw beef.

Listeria. The bacterium *Listeria monocytogenes* poses a risk to our most vulnerable populations—children, the elderly, and pregnant women—and exhibits a high mortality rate in those infected. A joint interagency risk assessment involving FSIS and CDC on *Listeria monocytogenes* contamination in retail facilities is underway through the application of a cross-contamination model. This risk assessment will inform decision-making about how to best address this pathogen in the retail setting, such as in deli counters at supermarkets. Moreover, there is significant scientific research sponsored by the food safety agencies that will help elucidate how to best prevent *Listeria* contamination at retail.

2. Improved Produce Safety

Salmonella and *E. coli* O157:H7 are also threats to the safety of fresh produce. According to FDA data, between 1996 and 2010, at least 131 foodborne illness outbreaks were associated with the consumption of fresh produce.

> Between 1996 and 2010, 131 foodborne illness outbreaks were associated with fresh produce.

In July 2009, building on experience gained through collaborative efforts with the produce industry, the FDA issued commodity-specific draft guidance on agricultural practices that can reduce the risk of microbial contamination in the production and distribution of tomatoes, melons, and leafy greens—three commodities that pose higher risk of such contamination than do other commodities. That draft guidance was intended to assist firms by recommending practices and preventive measures to minimize the microbial food safety hazards of the products throughout the entire supply chain and thereby create a minimum standard for production across the country.

> FDA issued draft guidance on the safe growing, handling and packing of tomatoes, melons and leafy greens.

FDA also committed in 2009 to establishing mandatory standards for safe growing practices that would build on its commodity-specific draft guidance and take account of the full diversity of the produce sector in terms of risk, growing practices and scale of operation. FDA has held listening sessions in thirteen states across the country to gather input for a new, comprehensive proposed rule to reduce the risk of

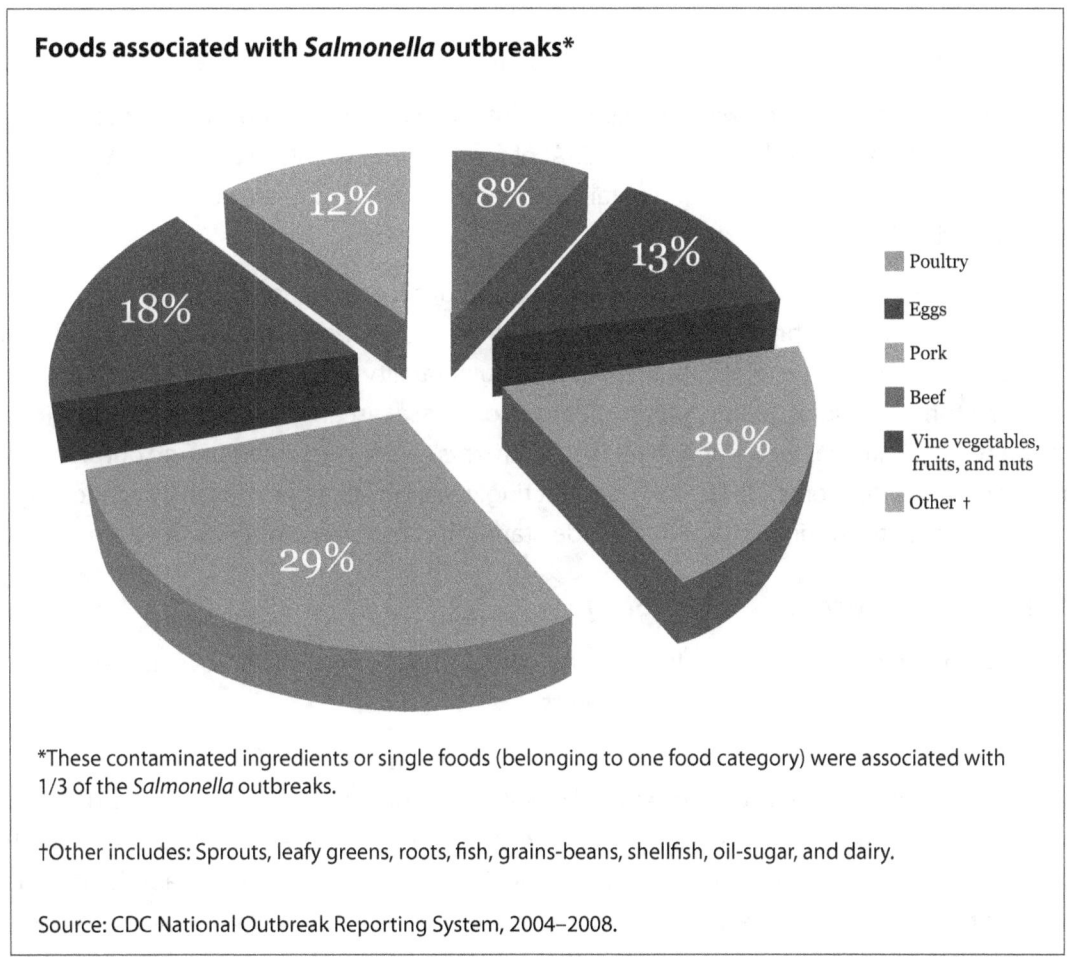

Foods associated with *Salmonella* outbreaks*

- Poultry: ngày 20%
- Eggs: 13%
- Pork: 8%
- Beef: 12%
- Vine vegetables, fruits, and nuts: 18%
- Other †: 29%

*These contaminated ingredients or single foods (belonging to one food category) were associated with 1/3 of the *Salmonella* outbreaks.

†Other includes: Sprouts, leafy greens, roots, fish, grains-beans, shellfish, oil-sugar, and dairy.

Source: CDC National Outbreak Reporting System, 2004–2008.

foodborne illnesses from the consumption of fresh produce through the implementation of preventive controls. Preventive controls for the produce industry will provide a consistent set of standards for the industry and reduce the risk of consuming contaminated produce.

> The Produce Safety Alliance was established to help produce growers and packers access materials that will help to improve food safety.

The Produce Safety Alliance, a three-year public-private partnership funded by FDA and USDA and housed at Cornell University, was established to help produce growers and packers access food safety education materials. This is a key step in preparation for new science-based standards for produce safety that are required by the Food Safety Modernization Act. Key activities of the alliance include: (1) Developing a standardized, but multi-formatted and multi-lingual education program on Good Agricultural Practices and co-management, (2) Creating an information bank of up-to-date scientific and technical information related to on-farm and packinghouse produce safety, (3) Launching a website to make the alliance's work and information readily accessible, and (4) Establishing a network of educational collaborators.

3. Preventing Intentional Adulteration

FSIS, FDA, and DHS collaborated with the National Center for Food Protection and Defense (NCFPD) to study economically motivated adulteration (EMA) of food products. Several potential EMA indicators were identified based on the information obtained. Quantitative measures are being developed to help identify potential EMA incidents.

FDA has also been working on several other fronts to improve food defense. First, FDA is working with major trade partners to improve global capacity to prevent intentional contamination and protect imports. Second, FDA is creating tools including: (a) vulnerability assessment software—agriculture and manufacturing modules; (b) mitigation strategies database—searchable by process step; (c) exercise kit for use by State and local public health departments to prepare for foodborne outbreaks, both unintentional and intentional. Third, FDA is conducting vulnerability assessments, using industry and academic expertise to continue to build our understanding of food systems to inform future efforts.

4. Other Preventive Measures in Food Safety

FSIS has issued several instructions to its inspection program personnel to improve the safety of meat and poultry produced at regulated establishments.

Residues. Residual drugs, pesticides, and environmental contaminants such as metals that are sometimes found in meat and poultry can pose a public health risk when found at certain levels. The National Residue Program (NRP), administered by FSIS, FDA, and EPA, is in place to protect the public from these residues. A newly formed Senior Executive Council has been charged with establishing Standard Operating Procedures (SOP) to review and improve the protocols of the NRP's sampling program, but foremost, to determine appropriate regulatory actions for cancelled pesticides and environmental contaminant residues. FSIS has also strengthened its enforcement activities by instructing its inspection program personnel to increase chemical residue testing in certain slaughter establishments that do not have an effective residue control program in place.

Allergens. In the first half of 2011, an increased number of products were recalled because of undeclared allergens or other ingredients, a significant public health concern due to the rising number of Americans sensitive to ingredients, such as milk, eggs, peanuts, tree nuts, soy, wheat, seafood and shellfish, that elicit potentially life-threatening responses.

FSIS inspectors were instructed to make establishments aware of the importance and prevalence of undeclared allergens in meat and poultry products, and how to best ensure labels are accurate and current.

> Under new FSIS proposed requirements, meat and poultry products would not be allowed to enter commerce until test results for harmful substances are received.

Test and hold. FSIS proposed a new requirement for the meat and poultry industry that, once enacted, will reduce the amount of unsafe food that reaches store shelves. With the proposed requirement, FSIS would be able to hold products from commerce until FSIS test results for harmful substances—such as *E. coli* O157:H7 and drug residues—are received. Currently, when FSIS collects a sample for testing, the sampled products are requested but not required to be held until test results are known. FSIS believes that this requirement will substantially reduce recalls for meat and poultry products.

Infant Formula. FDA is finalizing its rule on infant formula, which will establish new or updated requirements including the following: (1) current good manufacturing practices, including audits, (2) growth monitoring studies to ensure that infant formulas support healthy growth, (3) microbial testing for pathogens of concern and (4) recordkeeping.

B. Enhanced Food Safety Surveillance and Compliance

In addition to supporting greater efforts to prevent foodborne illness in the first place, the FSWG has also taken important steps to strengthen the capacity of the food safety system to monitor the cause of illnesses, detect emergent outbreaks as early as possible, and ensure compliance with food safety standards, with a special focus on improving oversight of imports.

> CDC has established seven FoodCORE sites which form a network of state and local health agencies that develop and implement best practices in outbreak investigations.

1. Disease surveillance

CDC has been working with state and local partners to achieve a comprehensive approach for foodborne illness surveillance that detects outbreaks; estimates illnesses, hospitalizations, and deaths; determines foods and settings causing illness; and tracks trends to determine whether control measures are working. For example, CDC works with public health partners to enhance the public health surveillance network for outbreak detection. Specifically, PulseNet, a national network of public health and food regulatory agency laboratories which is coordinated by the CDC, is now in all 50 states and 82 countries. PulseNet participants perform standardized molecular subtyping (or "fingerprinting") of foodborne disease-causing bacteria by pulsed-field gel electrophoresis (PFGE). PFGE can be used to distinguish strains of organisms, such as Escherichia coli O157:H7, Salmonella, Shigella, Listeria, or Campylobacter at the DNA level. PulseNet allows for rapid detection of foodborne disease case clusters and real-time communication among state, local health departments, and international partners, as well as facilitates early identification of common source outbreaks.

Additionally, the CaliciNet surveillance system for noroviruses is now operational in 25 states. In August 2010, CDC expanded FoodCORE (Foodborne Diseases Centers for Outbreak Repsonse Enhancement) following an initial pilot program, which was supported in part by FSIS. Seven sites are implementing work plans to build replicative models for enhanced outbreak response activities. Resources have already played a critical role in the rapid containment of several recent outbreaks, both single- and multi-state, including *E. coli* O157 and hazelnuts, and *Salmonella* in Lebanon bologna, chicken livers and queso fresco. FoodCORE resources facilitated rapid and comprehensive laboratory, epidemiologic, and environmental health response during these investigations.

CDC is meeting its obligations under the Food Safety and Modernization Act (FSMA) by establishing a Surveillance Working Group that consists of members of federal, state and local governments, academia, industry, and consumer groups. The Working Group met and offered guidance related to the designation of Food Safety Integrated Centers of Excellence, also mandated by FSMA. Future Working Group efforts will be focused on enhancements to foodborne diseases surveillance.

CDC launched a new web-based surveillance platform to enhance the speed and completeness of foodborne outbreak reports. CDC also developed an online database to make data more publicly accessible and better inform both detection and prevention efforts. In January 2011, CDC published revised and updated estimates of foodborne illnesses hospitalizations and deaths in the United States, which form the basis for future policies and research in food safety. In June, 2011, CDC published the FoodNet annual report card on food safety in the United States, showing that *E. coli* O157 infections have been reduced, but *Salmonella* infections have not declined in 15 years.

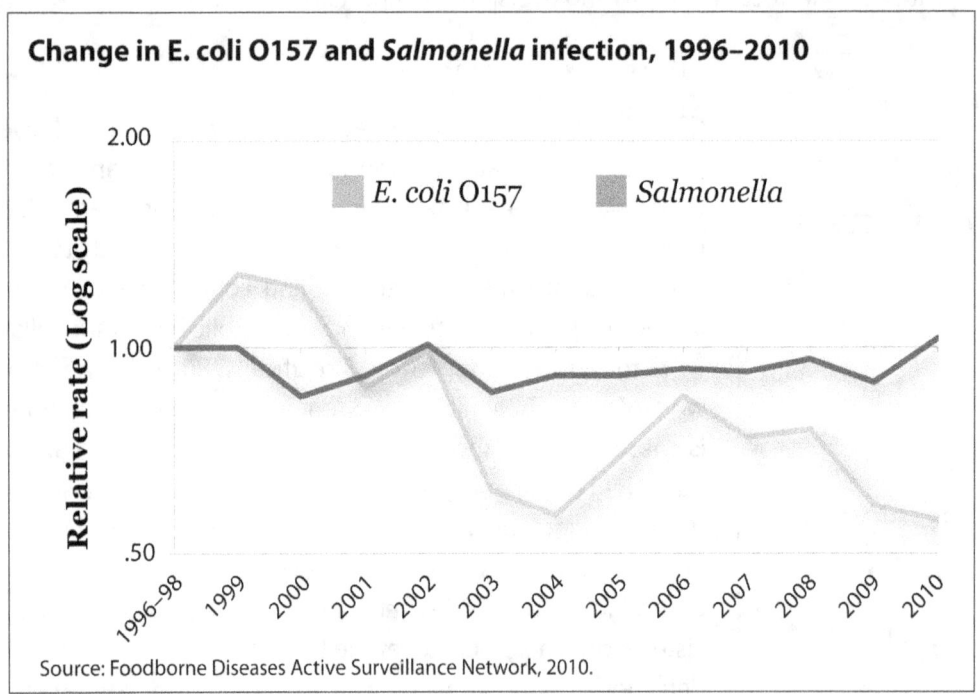

2. Reportable Food Registry

In September 2009, the FDA launched the congressionally-mandated electronic Reportable Food Registry (RFR) portal for industry and public health officials to report significant food safety incidents, such as contamination of food with pathogenic bacteria. Specifically, registered food facilities that manufacture, process, pack, or hold food for human or animal consumption in the United States under section 415(a) of the Food, Drug & Cosmetic Act are required to report when there is a reasonable probability that the use of, or exposure to, an article of food will cause serious adverse health consequences or death to humans or animals. Federal, state, and local government officials may voluntarily use the RFR portal to report information that may come to them about reportable foods.

FDA has received over 2240 RFR reports and has established new mechanisms for expedited evaluation and response so that swift action can be taken to protect consumers, typically in collaboration with

> FDA's Reportable Food Registry requires the food industry to file electronic reports about food safety problems. The registry has led to the recall of products that presented a risk due to *Salmonella*.

the reporting firm. For example, RFR reports enabled FDA to act swiftly to address the presence of *Salmonella* in hydrolyzed vegetable protein, prepared foods containing undeclared sulfites, and glass in animal feed.

In 2011, FDA issued the first annual report on the RFR entitled, "A New Approach to Targeting Inspection Resources and Identifying Patterns of Adulteration," covering results from September 2009 through September 2010. The report demonstrates that, in its first year, the RFR significantly strengthened the ability of the FDA to track patterns of food and feed adulteration and target inspection resources to identify adulterated food/feed and prevent foodborne illnesses.

3. Antimicrobial Resistance

Foodborne pathogens that infect humans have become increasingly resistant to antimicrobial drugs, posing significant healthcare challenges when foodborne illness in humans requires treatment with those drugs. In order to address this problem, FDA, CDC and USDA participate in the National Antimicrobial Resistance Monitoring System (NARMS), a national public health surveillance system that tracks antibiotic resistance in foodborne bacteria. The most recent joint executive report on NARMS was published by FDA, CDC and USDA/ARS in May 2011. This report focuses on pathogens from food animals, retail meats and human clinical cases, based on data through 2008, and will provide a basis to inform and create scientifically sound solutions to public health and food safety concerns involving antimicrobial resistance.

The bacteria currently under surveillance by NARMS include: *Salmonella, Campylobacter, Escherichia coli,* and *Enterococcus*. NARMS monitors trends in antimicrobial resistance among foodborne bacteria from humans, retail meats, and animals; disseminates timely information on antimicrobial resistance to promote interventions that reduce resistance among foodborne bacteria; conducts research to better understand the emergence, persistence, and spread of antimicrobial resistance; and assists in making decisions related to the approval of safe and effective antimicrobial drugs for animals.

In addition to monitoring antimicrobial susceptibility, NARMS partners collaborate on epidemiologic and microbiologic research studies and examine foodborne bacteria for genetic relatedness, using pulsed-field gel electrophoresis (PFGE). NARMS also collaborates with antimicrobial resistance monitoring systems in other countries to work towards international harmonization of testing and reporting.

4. Import Safety

Food imports are growing rapidly and now comprise 15 percent of the total U.S. food supply, with much higher portions being imported in key categories, including: seafood (75-80 percent), fresh fruit (about 50 percent) and vegetables (about 20 percent).

FDA, FSIS, CDC, and U.S. Customs and Border Protection (CBP) have made significant efforts to improve U.S. oversight and ultimately the safety of imported food, including better targeting and data sharing at ports of entry, enhanced collaboration with foreign regulatory counterparts, and food safety capacity building where it is most needed in countries exporting to the United States.

In October 2010, several agencies entered into the Commercial Targeting and Analysis Center (CTAC) to expand access to import data. In addition, an Interagency Policy Coordination (IPC) committee was established by agency leadership as a part of the signed agreement on "Principles of Import." Three priorities have been identified by the IPC, including the Sea/Rail Manifest (document imaging), Cargo Control and Release (interface with PHIS), and the National Export Initiative of March 2010. Also, the U.S. Customs and Border Protection (CBP) has identified aggressive project schedules for the interim solutions over the next few months, which will enable shipments to be held at manifest level, receive documents through portal access to ACE, and interface with CBP's current IT system to enable data exchange when the entry is filed. In addition to the activities of this IPC, the FSIS will continue active involvement in the ACE/ITDS interim solutions.

> PREDICT allows FDA to target shipments of imported food that are likely to pose the greatest risk, enabling FDA to screen more than 10 million import entries each year.

FDA has developed and made significant progress in implementing a computer-based, data-driven tool for targeting examinations of imported food shipments, called PREDICT (Predictive, Risk-based Evaluation for Dynamic Import Compliance Targeting). This tool enables FDA to screen the over 10 million import entries of food commodities entering the U.S. annually to identify the ones most likely to pose a food safety risk or be in non-compliance with U.S. standards. PREDICT enables FDA to better protect food safety and make best use of its resources.

The food safety agencies have also strengthened international capacity and fostered cooperation with international partners to reduce global threats. The FDA continues to work closely with other countries, with a particular focus on those that export large volumes of foods to the United States. FDA also established a Joint Committee on Food Safety with its partner agencies in Canada (CFIA and Health Canada) to develop strategies to ensure the safety of our respective food supplies. FDA also continues to work closely with the appropriate entities in Mexico, including frequent communications on produce safety. The U.S. Deputy Commissioner for Foods visited China, the European Union, Canada and Mexico and continues to work to strengthen ties with these trading partners. The FDA foreign offices also foster critical communication and coordination on food safety efforts in China, India, Latin America, the Middle East and Africa. In 2009, the CDC began providing training to epidemiologists in Central America to improve their ability to estimate the burden of foodborne illness,

> The food safety agencies have also strengthened international capacity and fostered cooperation with international partners to reduce global threats.

improve *Salmonella* surveillance and improve laboratory capacity in order to improve their own food supply, and reduce threats to the safety of foods which are likely to enter the global market. In April 2011, FSIS participated in a Central American Customs Union (CACU) workshop in El Salvador presenting information on product registration and export certification, as well as microbiological standards for meat products with particular emphasis on *Salmonella* and other pathogens. The regional workshop engaged the CACU countries of Costa Rica, El Salvador, Guatemala, Honduras and Nicaragua in crucial discussions of its own 2009 food safety standards. Their regulation seeks to establish the microbiological parameters and permissible limits for the registration and sanitary surveillance of food products and its provisions apply to all food products marketed in Central American countries.

CDC and FDA continue to be involved with and supportive of the important work of Global Foodborne Infection Network (formerly Global Salm Surv), INFOSAN, FERG, and other key World Health Organization (WHO) activities that support global food safety. For instance, in 2011, WHO Global Foodborne Infection Network held seven training courses in six countries. Each course brings together microbiologists and epidemiologists to learn methods for outbreak surveillance, and isolation, identification, and serotyping of various foodborne pathogens. In June 2009, the FDA established an agreement with the WHO for a global information platform and continues to develop a broad cooperative agreement between FDA and the WHO to coordinate work more efficiently.

The FDA has also developed the International Comparability Assessment Tool (ICAT) and a process for evaluating a foreign country's overall food safety regulatory system. From May through September of 2010, the ICAT and comparability process was piloted with New Zealand, which included extensive document review and on-site verification audits. A similar exercise began with the European Union in early 2011.

In December 2009, the FDA ran a third-party audit pilot program in shrimp processing facilities, many of which operate overseas. That program gave the FDA an opportunity to gather technical and operational information on facility compliance from third party auditors in order to develop evaluation tools and assess the utility of that information. The program also helped FDA assess the infrastructure needs for recognizing and managing third-party certification systems, gain knowledge of types of certification programs currently used by industry, and assess the implementation of certification programs against FDA's needs and expectations.

To further improve food safety practices in countries exporting to the United States, FDA, FSIS, the USDA Foreign Agricultural Service, and U.S. Codex office have created the International Policy Coordination Group (IPCG). The IPCG assesses ongoing U.S. Government (USG) international food safety technical assistance and capacity building activities, to develop a coordinated USG approach to developing and implementing future activities, and to consider future coordinated approaches to selected food safety issues facing developing countries and emerging markets. The IPCG is working on the transition from a forum for reacting to regulatory non-compliance to one of providing technical assistance focused on developing food safety systems, the operational principles for successful technical assistance, and current/future models to deliver effective programs. In addition, the IPCG is supporting the establishment of a unified International Food Safety Forum to help U.S. leadership work effectively with foreign counterparts to improve food safety internationally.

C. Food Safety Response

While much can be done to improve prevention, the highly complex and decentralized nature of the food supply system makes some occurrence of foodborne illness inevitable and impossible to eradicate completely. A sound food safety system depends on the quick and efficacious response to an outbreak once detected. Here, too, the FSWG agencies have taken important steps to increase the system's ability to respond to outbreaks of foodborne illness.

1. Strengthening the National Traceback and Response System

Creating a Coordinated Incident Command System. To facilitate communication and decision-making during outbreaks of foodborne illness, in 2010, HHS and USDA established an "Incident Command System Working Group" that developed protocols for a Multi-Agency Coordination Group for Foodborne Illness Outbreaks. This Coordination Group can quickly convene during an outbreak of foodborne illness involving multiple federal agencies to share information, make decisions, and leverage resources. In addition, outbreak response managers from CDC, FDA, and FSIS have been actively working together over the past two years to improve communications and coordination during outbreaks. FSIS and FDA have embedded epidemiologists in CDC's foodborne outbreak detection and response section to improve information flow among the agencies, especially during the early stages of an outbreak.

FDA has invested in a multi-tiered approach for the development and implementation of an effective NIMS Incident Command System. In order to promote the application of ICS principles within the agency and its federal, state, and local agency partners, FDA has delivered 27 classroom trainings of intermediate ICS 300 with a total of 753 personnel trained (694 FDA, 58 State personnel and one DHS) and 23 classroom training of advanced ICS 400 with a total of 592 personnel trained (571 FDA, 56 State personnel and one DHS), since mid-FY2008. Since March 2010, FDA has completed 8 sessions of ICS 402, providing an ICS overview for 109 Executives/Senior Officials within the agency. FDA has also delivered classroom position-specific training to a total of 105 personnel, including Incident Commanders, Operations Section Chiefs, Planning Section Chiefs, Logistics Section Chiefs and Finance/Admin Section Chiefs who are targeted to convene Incident Management Teams (IMTs) that will be expected to mobilize/deploy in a response capacity.

Updating Emergency Operations Procedures and Outbreak Response. An effective outbreak response requires quicker and better communication and coordination among federal, state, and local agencies. Since July 2009, CDC has expanded its partnership with state and local health departments to coordinate aggressive and rapid investigations of numerous major multistate outbreaks. These investigations have identified major hazards that required large recalls, such as the outbreak of *Salmonella* infections in 2010 that led to the recall of half a billion shell eggs, unexpected food vehicles, such as frozen microwaveable dinners, mamey fruit pulp, and Gouda cheese, and a new foodborne pathogen (Shiga-toxin producing *E. coli* O145, which was linked to shredded lettuce). In August 2009, the federal food safety agencies issued a letter to state and local agencies in

> A sound food safety system depends on the quick and efficacious response to an outbreak once detected.

support of the Council to Improve Foodborne Outbreak Response's (CIFOR) *Guidelines for Foodborne Disease Outbreak Response*. A CIFOR Guidelines Toolkit was published that will enable state and local jurisdictions to conduct a self-evaluation of their foodborne disease outbreak detection and response procedures and to identify recommendations in the CIFOR *Guidelines* that can improve their procedures. CDC funded 15 states and 4 local jurisdictions with small training grants that enabled their foodborne disease outbreak response team members to use the *Toolkit* to self-assess and identify appropriate recommendations from the *Guidelines*. Due to the popularity of these *Toolkit* trainings, another RFP has been issued to fund additional state and local *Toolkit* trainings. The *Toolkit* has been distributed to all states and to all CIFOR member organizations and is available on the CIFOR website. In addition, FDA continues to work with State and local agencies to build food safety infrastructure nationally through the Integrated Federal-State Food Safety System effort.

FDA enhanced its role in outbreak response and prevention with the launch of the Coordinated Outbreak Response and Evaluation (CORE) Network. Staffed by experts in epidemiology, consumer complaints, statistics and veterinary medicine, the CORE Network is managing surveillance, response and post-response activities related to incidents of illness linked to FDA-regulated human and animal food. CORE's goals are to streamline decision-making, respond more quickly to outbreaks and ensure seamless coordination and enhanced communication. The team will also standardize post-response activities such as environmental assessments and root cause analyses, which provide an opportunity to learn what went wrong and use that information to drive strategies to prevent outbreaks from occurring in the future.

> FDA launched the CORE Network, a multi-disciplinary team that manages surveillance, response and post-response activities related to illness incidents.

Since 2003, CDC has funded the National Environmental Health Association to conduct four Epi-Ready Foodborne Disease Outbreak Team Training courses per year for local and state environmental health specialists, laboratorians, and epidemiologists. USDA has provided funding for live, interactive broadcasts of several of these Epi-Ready courses to remote sites that greatly increased the reach of the training. FDA staff have served as trainers as well as helping to guide the course content. The food safety agencies have also promoted a more highly trained environmental health workforce, which is skilled in properly conducting an environmental assessment during foodborne illness investigations. In total, more than 2,400 students from all 50 states have gone through Epi-Ready training.

In October 2009, the FDA expanded its federal-state Rapid Response Teams (RRT) project to help local and State partners work with FDA partners to identify and implement systems that strengthen existing state food safety programs and develop capabilities for coordinated and rapid responses to food-related incidents and emergencies. In FY 2010, the RRTs participated in an annual face-to-face meeting involving 80 participants from 40 federal and state offices. Meeting participants shared capabilities and spent time developing and harmonizing project directions. Since the meeting, the RRTs have formed working groups to develop a documentation of best practices in the development of key response capabilities. These documents include various measures that are being developed into metrics of capacity and achievement. Each working group completed a draft chapter for an "RRT Playbook" of rapid response capabilities, including the chapters on topics such as "Working with Other Agencies," "Communication Standard Operating Procedures (SOPs)," and "Joint Inspections."

Developing Industry Product Tracing Systems. Despite the dedicated efforts of food safety officials across the country, the existing capacity to traceback the sources of illness is limited. Public and private sector officials often lack rapid access to information about the sources of foods or ingredients, making the traceback process more cumbersome and leading to less-accurately targeted recalls. In addition, multiple federal, state, and local agencies all play essential roles in managing outbreaks, but lack a unified structure or adequate systems for sharing traceback data in an emergency. These limitations make it essential for Federal agencies to improve the traceability of food and the response to outbreaks of foodborne illness. In order to correct these problems, FDA has completed a pilot study on tracing with the tomato industry to devise more rapid and efficient ways to trace problems to their source. FDA and FSIS hosted public meetings on product tracing to identify steps the food industry can take to establish systems to improve our national capacity for detecting the origins of foodborne illnesses, and are currently reviewing comments received from the public meetings. In addition, FDA announced in September 2011 that the Institute of Food Technologists (IFT) will carry out two new pilot projects aimed at enhancing the agency's and industry's ability to trace products responsible for foodborne illness outbreaks. The pilots will evaluate methods and technologies for rapid and effective tracing of foods, including types of data that are useful for tracing, ways to connect the various points in the supply chain, and how quickly the data are made available to the FDA.

2. Recalls

FSIS revised the recall process to provide information to consumers more directly and clearly. The word "voluntary" was removed from recall communications to ensure consumers do not underestimate the seriousness of a recall. FDA and FSIS also collaborated on a mobile application for smart phones to provide consumers instant access to food recalls, alerts, and to view picture of labels. This application was launched by the White House in 2010, as a part of a product recall app, and can be accessed on USA.gov. In two recent outbreaks, inter-agency and industry collaboration provided consumers with a source to learn information about all of the recalled products so they could make informed food purchase and disposal decisions.

In order to broadly improve communication to the public regarding food safety, CDC, FDA and FSIS launched an enhanced and updated food safety website, "www.foodsafety.gov," in September 2009. The website also provides a mechanism for rapid information dissemination and alerts to consumers about food recalls.

> FERN—the Food Emergency Response Network—provides additional laboratory capacity during large-scale events. Recent incidents where FERN has played a role include *E. coli* in spinach and the oil spill.

D. Additional Agency Coordination, Capacity Building, and Partnerships

Partnerships among federal agencies, state, local, tribal, and territorial entities, academia, and private partners are crucial to enhancing the safety of the food supply.

Laboratory practices and capacity are key areas for inter-agency collaboration. FSIS, FDA and CDC have had ongoing technical exchanges to promote strategies for rapid detection of *Salmonella* in food products and emerging technologies for molecular sub-typing methods. These efforts are coordinated with industry to more effectively characterize pathogens during outbreak investigations. FSIS and the Food Emergency Response Network (FERN) laboratories have developed and established national standards for laboratory qualifications for detection of pathogens in food involving 37 federal agencies; 116 state and 17 local laboratories; and signed 30 cooperative laboratory agreements. FDA developed a Partnership for Food Protection (PFP) workgroup to develop national laboratory standards to address consistency of findings among state laboratories.

FSIS and FDA are also assisting state food testing laboratories in obtaining accreditation under ISO Standard 17025, the gold standard for food-testing laboratories. This is part of a multi-year effort to create additional opportunities to identify means to protect public health. In addition, the FERN is equipped to provide supplemental laboratory analytical and surge capacity during large-scale events, both natural and man-made. FERN has been successfully activated during several recent incidents including melamine, *E. coli* O157:H7 in spinach, and the oil spill. FDA has established "High Throughput Laboratories" that cover the areas of Chemistry, Microbiology, Drugs and Environmental Samples. These laboratories have established capabilities to handle larger volumes of samples in shorter time-frames without compromising quality or integrity. Development also continues on the FDA Laboratory Information System (LIMS) initiative, under the Automated Lab Management (ALM) Program, to provide an automated system to manage and automate laboratory operations throughout all 13 FDA field and 2 mobile laboratories.

In FY 2011, FDA established Vet-LRN, the Veterinary-Laboratory Response Network, which includes state and federal laboratories that integrate resources and expertise for timely and accurate reporting, identification, and analysis of animal feed chemical and microbiological contamination events. The system operates by examining animal tissues and diagnostic specimens for microbiological agents, toxins, and other causes of disease. The Center for Veterinary Medicine provides early detection of pet food borne disease outbreaks with rapid notification to stakeholders in order to minimize animal illness and related economic loss. These efforts contribute to overall food safety as animal feed events could signal potential issues in the human food system.

In March 2011, Vet-LRN held its first developmental meeting with veterinary laboratory directors from around the U.S. and Canada. The goal of the meeting was to establish contact with various laboratories that are interested in joining the network. Comments and ideas were provided by the laboratory directors to help Vet-LRN plan its activities and coordinate with other existing networks such as the Food Emergency Response Network and other animal disease health networks in the United States such as USDA's National Animal Health Laboratory Network.

CDC continues to strengthen PulseNet, the national molecular subtyping network for foodborne disease surveillance which has revolutionized the detection and investigation of foodborne disease outbreaks. This network of local, state, territorial, agricultural and federal laboratories in 50 states and 82 countries is coordinated by CDC and the Association of Public Health Laboratories.

Beyond laboratory collaborations, several forums have been created or reconfigured to better enable agency coordination. For instance, CDC, FDA and FSIS convened an interagency outbreak response working group to clarify roles and interactions among agencies during outbreak response activities. This effort led to earlier and routine communications among agencies in outbreak detection, and a program to provide cross-training of staff among agencies.

> CDC strengthened PulseNet, the foodborne disease surveillance network spanning 50 states and 82 countries.

The Interagency Risk Assessment Consortium (IRAC) has been restructured to serve as the coordinating council to develop and oversee the conduct of joint FDA-FSIS-CDC risk assessments. The IRAC includes membership from 19 federal agencies and sub-agencies and meets quarterly to review progress in accomplishing annual goals on specific topic areas and activities relevant to food-safety risk assessments. This includes developing risk assessment modeling methodology, engaging in data collection and analysis, and providing interagency peer review of risk assessments.

Another forum, the Food Safety Working Group Information Technology Task Force (ITTF), was established to develop recommendations for achieving greater interoperability and harmonizing electronic data collection standards between the agencies and State and local authorities. Utilizing a useful crowd-sourcing tool, IdeaJam, the ITTF developed 41 initial recommendations, thereby fulfilling its charge and eventually agreeing to implement 15 final recommendations approved by the CDC, EPA, FSIS, and FDA.

In August 2010, FDA hosted a 50-state workshop entitled "A United Approach to Public Health" to facilitate greater progress toward the creation of an integrated national food safety system. Building upon the 2008 workshop, where ten working groups were formed under the Partnership for Food Protection (PFP), this workshop highlighted the progress of the PFP workgroups. These workgroups consisted of Response, Training, Interactive Information Technology, and Risk-Based Work Planning; and the FDA/Center for Veterinary Medicine-led Pet Event Tracking Network (PETNet) project. The Partnership for Food Protection Coordinating Committee is currently looking at the recommendations made by the 50-state breakout groups and is evaluating how best to integrate the suggestions to improve the design and implementation of an Integrated Food Safety System.

E. Retail Food Safety

In September 2011, FDA announced a Retail Food Safety Action Plan that includes several measures to help assure the safety of food sold in food stores, restaurants, schools, and other foodservice operations in the United States. The Action Plan focuses on improving the way managers of these establishments conduct food safety operations in their facilities, as well as improving the oversight of these establishments by public health agencies at the federal, state and local levels. The Plan specifically calls for strengthening State and local food safety requirements that apply to these establishments and for improving training for personnel on measures to keep food safe.

F. Consumer Education

While those involved in the commercial production, processing, distribution and retail sale of food have a primary obligation to do everything they reasonably can to prevent food safety problems, consumers also contribute to prevention by observing proper food handling practices. The federal government is enhancing its support for food safety education that enables consumers to better understand and play their food safety role.

To further engage consumers and educate them about the importance of food safety in the kitchen, USDA, in collaboration with FDA and CDC, launched an Ad Council advertising campaign to educate consumers about safe food handling practices. This Food Safe Families campaign is a national, multi-media effort utilizing television, radio, print and online advertising designed to fulfill the agencies' responsibility to raise awareness of foodborne illness and provide consumers with information they need to practice safe food handling behaviors. The ads urge consumers to learn more at http://www.foodsafety.gov—a redesigned and vastly expanded inter-agency website which hosts vital food safety information on safe handling behaviors and recall information. This unprecedented campaign exemplifies inter-agency cooperation. The campaign also benefited from input of the Ad Council's Expert Panel which included a vast array of stakeholders all along the farm to table continuum including producers, industry and consumer groups, retailers, academics and public health professionals.

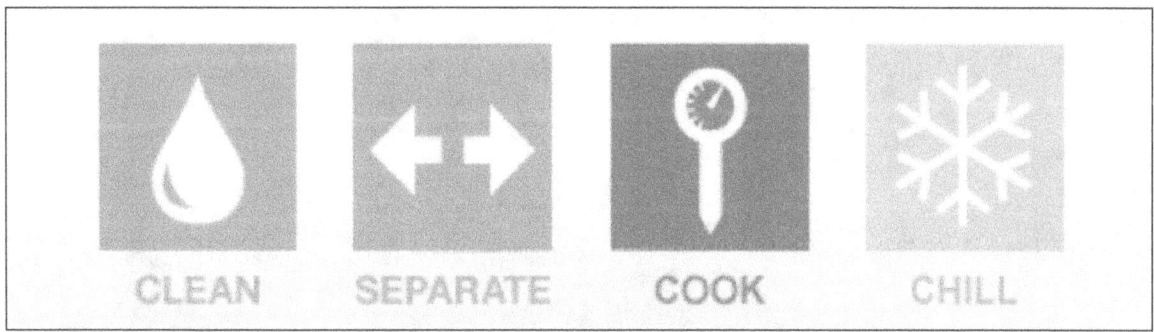

The FDA awarded the Partnership for Food Safety Education (PFSE) a sole-source grant to support a strategic planning process to determine future directions and strategies for food safety education. Through the strategic planning process, technical experts have examined the scientific underpinnings of current messages, while social scientists have examined strategies for creating behavior change. PFSE is a not-for-profit organization that unites industry associations, professional societies, consumer groups, academia and government to educate the public about safe food handling.

FDA also conducted its 12th annual, week-long training session for science teachers based on its *Science and Our Food Supply* curriculum. Science teachers learn the fundamental science critical to food safety and perform the curriculum laboratories. They return to their schools around the country and teach students important safe food handling measures to prevent illness and educate them on the science of food safety. The training was developed in cooperation with the National Science Teachers Association. Since the program began, the curriculum has reached about 4 million students nationwide. In addition, FSIS and FDA updated a series of new brochures for populations who have been identified as having at greater risk of foodborne illness and posted on its web site two videos for consumers on the safe handling of seafood and fresh produce.

FSIS conducted consumer focus-group studies in 2010 to measure consumer understanding of labeling regarding the safe handling and preparation of meat, poultry, and egg products. Participants provided useful information on their lack of understanding of labeling information. The findings of this focus group study can be used in the future to improve decisions about labeling and to better develop a consumer survey that could then be generalized to the consumer population.

CDC's new *Vital Signs* is a monthly report on a single, important public health topic. In June, 2011 the *Vital Signs* report focused on Food Safety. The report was led by CDC's Foodborne Diseases Active Surveillance Network (FoodNet) program and was a coordinated effort with FDA and USDA. The data highlights the success in reducing *E. coli* O157 infections, while pointing out that *Salmonella* infections have not declined in 15 years. The report takes consumers through the steps along the farm-to-table continuum and shows what needs to be targeted for action everywhere food is grown (production), made (manufactured), moved (transportation), prepared (in restaurants, grocery stores, and homes), and consumed. The report ends with an important Call to Action for everyone who is involved in food safety and points to FoodSafety.gov as a gateway to information for consumers, including a blog on *Salmonella*. The report was released in the midst of the *E.coli* O104 outbreak in Europe, calling even more attention to this important public health concern, and reached over 684 million people within 48 hours.

(Source: http://www.foodsafety.gov/keep/basics)

II. Food Safety Working Group 2011-12 Agenda and Beyond

The FSWG's accomplishments to date represent a large down payment on a stronger food safety system that will deliver greater value, better prevent illnesses and more effectively promote the well-being of the American people. Building on those efforts, the FSWG will continue to strengthen the food safety system through increased prevention, enhanced surveillance, and faster response. It will do so in part through implementing the new FDA Food Safety Modernization Act (FSMA).

During 2010, the FSWG's member agencies worked closely with the Administration, Congress, and key stakeholders on this critical legislation. The FSMA provides a new vision and mandate for the food safety system, focused on science-based prevention of food safety problems and risk-based targeting of public and private prevention efforts to get the most risk reduction "bang for the buck."

To carry out this vision, Congress has directed FDA to establish new prevention oriented standards for the food industry, provided new inspection and enforcement tools to ensure high rates of compliance with those standards, and mandated the creation of a new system of import oversight so that imported food meets the same modern standards as domestically-produced food. FSMA also calls for FDA to work in close partnership with other federal agencies, to build a nationally integrated system of inspection and laboratory testing with state and local partners, and to work closely with foreign governments to improve import safety. In addition, Congress has directed CDC to strengthen and enhance public health surveillance and response systems in partnership with state and local health departments and to designate Centers of Excellence which will provide additional resources for frontline health professionals during outbreaks and conduct research and outreach activities regarding food safety.

The FSMA presents a significant opportunity and challenge for our food safety agencies. Implementation of this new legislation will be one of the highest priorities for the FSWG and its members over the next several years.

A. Greater Prevention

The federal food safety agencies will build on past prevention efforts and harness the new mandates of the FSMA to strengthen prevention of foodborne illness.

1. Pre-Harvest Food Safety

FSIS, FDA and CDC have a common interest in working with the scientific, agricultural and public health communities to solve the problem of infection and transmission of foodborne disease organisms at the point of livestock and fresh produce production. For example, while *E. coli* O157:H7 emerged as a hazard in beef in the early 1990s, the pathogen is now a significant cause of illness associated with fresh produce as well. While FSIS will continue implementing the FSWG recommendation to increase enforcement in beef facilities and FDA will issue rules for grower practices affecting produce safety, FSIS and its partner agencies at USDA will work with other federal agencies, producers, and scientists to discuss

> **Next Steps:**
>
> FDA will require preventive food safety controls for food and feed facilities and produce.

how to minimize pathogen contamination in animal production. FSIS and other USDA agencies will take the lead in conducting a thorough review and assessment of pre-harvest activities in the industry and government and engage stakeholders to consider initiatives in the areas of research, incentives for technology development and adoption, and identification and dissemination of best practices.

USDA convened a public meeting in November among FSIS, the Animal and Plant Health Inspection Service (APHIS), and the Agricultural Research Service (ARS) to discuss how pre-harvest pathogen control strategies for animals presented for slaughter can reduce the likelihood that beef could become contaminated with Shiga toxin-producing E. coli, Salmonella, and other pathogens. The meeting featured presentations on the latest research, followed by workshop discussions that included a wide variety of stakeholder groups. After analyzing the public comments presented at the meeting, USDA intends to convene a second public meeting focused on pre-harvest pathogen control strategies for poultry.

2. Upcoming Preventive Control Standards

As mandated by the FSMA, FDA will issue new rules establishing preventive control requirements for produce growers, food and animal feed processing facilities, and food transporters, as well as to prevent intentional adulteration of food over the next one to three years. FDA has done significant outreach with stakeholders to prepare for the issuance of these rules. It held a series of three public meetings to inform interested parties of the agency's current thinking regarding preventive controls, import oversight, and inspection and compliance and to solicit comment from stakeholders. The public meeting on preventive controls, in particular, gave stakeholders an opportunity to hear about FDA's thinking on preventive controls for food and feed facilities and produce safety standards. This public meeting complemented the listening tours with farmers that FDA undertook in 2010 and 2011 in thirteen states to understand the complexities of the produce industry prior to developing a regulation. FDA is working towards a release of proposed regulations on preventive controls for food and feed facilities, produce safety standards, and a foreign supplier verification program to ensure that importers are verifying compliance with these standards for imported foods. FDA will work with USDA and other Administration partners to ensure that the final standards take into account the full diversity and complexity of these sectors.

FDA has also recently established a National Food Safety Preventive Controls Alliance and an industry-oriented food safety training program to assist the US food industry in complying with regulations promulgated in response to FSMA legislation. The objectives of the National Food Safety Preventive Control Alliance include:

- To provide food facilities in the US with the resources to be in compliance with the preventive control component of FSMA.

- To assist the FDA to disseminate the science and technical elements relevant to the hazard analysis and preventive controls aspects of FSMA legislation to the US food industry.
- To assist the US food industry, particularly the small and medium-sized companies, to be compliant with the FSMA legislation.

For egg safety, FSIS is developing a proposed rule to address food safety risks in the egg products industry and will require Hazard Analysis and Critical Control Point (HACCP) systems in every establishment that produces egg products. By applying new standards, the egg product industry will be expected to comply with a system similar to that for meat and poultry products. FDA will continue to implement its prevention-based regulations for shell eggs.

3. Retail Food Safety

The federal agencies participating in FSWG have several proposed rules and other initiatives underway that will have a significant impact on retail food safety. For instance, within the coming year, FDA will improve retail food safety by encouraging more uniform state adoption of FDA's recommended standards for retail food safety, strengthening state and local inspection programs, and increasing the presence of certified food safety managers in retail facilities in accordance with its Retail Food Safety Action Plan. FSIS will publish a new regulation to revise its inspection procedures to ensure they are better focused on public health protection. FDA, FSIS and CDC are working on a risk assessment on *Listeria monocytogenes* that specifically addresses retail practices. In preparation for this risk assessment, a *Federal Register* notice requesting scientific data was published and the agencies held a public meeting. In addition the agencies are working through CDC's Environmental Health Specialists Network (EHS-Net) program and engaging in collaborative research with industry and academic partners to develop supporting data.

> **Next Steps:**
>
> FDA will improve retail food safety by:
>
> 1. Encouraging more uniform state adoption of FDA standards;
>
> 2. Strengthening state and local inspection programs; and
>
> 3. Increasing the presence of certified food safety managers in retail facilities.

B. Enhanced Surveillance and Compliance

1. Domestic Inspection and Compliance

Under the FSMA, FDA will be modernizing its approach to food safety inspection to take advantage of the preventive control framework and make better use of scarce inspection resources. The primary focus will shift from looking for problems in food safety facilities and correcting them after the fact to verifying that facility operators are implementing well-planned and documented systems for preventing problems. This approach is more effective and efficient because it helps ensure that proper practices are being observed on a continuing basis.

> **Next Steps:**
>
> Food importers will be responsible for providing documented assurances to FDA that the food they import has been produced under the same prevention-oriented standards as domestic food.

FDA will also begin using the new administrative enforcement powers granted by the FSMA to prevent food safety problems. This includes administratively detaining products that have been produced under substandard conditions that jeopardize safety and suspending the registration and thus ability to operate facilities whose food products are putting consumers at risk due to inappropriate practices. When necessary, FDA will also use its new power to mandate recalls of foods that are contaminated or linked with illness outbreaks.

2. Import Safety

FDA will focus on implementing the new import safety tool kit Congress created with the enactment of FSMA. Under the new system, food importers will be responsible for providing documented assurances to FDA that the food they import has been produced under the same prevention-oriented standards as domestic food. FDA will be able to verify the adequacy of the assurances by examining the importer's records and selectively examining import shipments. FDA will also support and supplement the efforts of importers by establishing an accredited third-party certification program, working with foreign governments and assessing the adequacy of food safety oversight and practices in countries exporting to the United Sates, and conducting inspections of foreign food facilities. Finally, FDA will implement a system to expedite entry of food shipments for importers that have especially well-documented systems to ensure safety.

FSIS has been working to further define its risk-based methodology for audits of equivalent countries allowed to export product to the U.S. FSIS will publish a document that details a performance-based approach to audits of foreign countries and point-of-entry re-inspections. This documentation will ensure that foreign equivalence audits continue to move in the direction of a risk-based approach and focus resources in an effective and efficient manner.

Federal agencies will continue working to ensure that foreign governments have the technical expertise and understanding of U.S. requirements that they need to be effective food safety partners.

3. Foodborne Illness Surveillance and Incident Investigation

As funding becomes available, CDC will maintain, upgrade and expand the PulseNet, and other subtyping networks, with more participants and next-generation methods to make outbreak detection and investigation faster and more robust for more pathogens. For example, CDC is developing new methods to deploy in state health department laboratories that will rapidly identify and subtype the important non-O157 Shiga toxin-producing *E. coli*, such as the one that caused a large and deadly outbreak in Germany in 2011. FoodCORE will evaluate the impact of enhanced outbreak response activities so that the most successful methods can be adopted by other state and local health departments. The proportion of foodborne illness that can be attributed to specific food commodities will be estimated based on reported foodborne outbreaks. In addition, CDC will launch a new FoodNet case-control study of risk factors for infection with non-O157 Shiga toxin producing *E. coli* and will complete a study of risk factors for developing hemolytic uremic syndrome among persons with *E. coli* O157:H7 infections.

In order to improve prevention and surveillance efforts, food safety programs need additional and new information on contributing factors and environmental antecedents of foodborne illness outbreaks. Currently, this information is lacking. A national voluntary environmental assessment information system could provide food-safety program managers with an information resource that could fill this gap. As a way to foster wider use of environmental assessments of farms and facilities to identify possible pathways of contamination, the National Voluntary Environmental Assessment Information System (NVEAIS) will be launched next year. CDC, as the lead agency, will continue to work with FSIS, FDA, state EHS-Net sites, and membership of the Conference for Food Protection to develop and implement the system. Information collected through NVEAIS will be used to establish a detailed characterization of food vehicles and monitor food vehicle trends, identify and monitor contributing factors and their environmental antecedents, and provide a basis for hypothesis generation regarding factors that may contribute to foodborne outbreak events. With this information, food safety programs and the food industry will have data to guide the planning, implementation and evaluation of foodborne illness prevention activities.

> **Next Steps:**
> CDC will maintain, upgrade and expand the PulseNet and similar networks with next-generation methods to make outbreak detection and investigation faster and more robust for more pathogens.

With support from FDA, FSIS, the National Park Service and EHS-Net states, CDC has also developed a virtual-world training program on how to conduct foodborne illness outbreak environmental assessments. This training program will be one of several requirements for participation in NVEAIS.

4. Product Tracing

FSIS relies heavily on records maintained by industry to identify trace back and trace forward on FSIS-regulated products associated with foodborne illness and other food safety incidents. Retail records are a critical component in trace back and trace forward activities, and are essential to quickly and effectively determine source product and ensure controls are enhanced by affected product manufacturers (e.g., official establishment, retail, foodservice). Yet, recent outbreak investigations were impeded by poor retail records.[1] FSIS will propose a rule to enhance access to records to facilitate trace back in case an illness or outbreak is associated with ground beef from retail stores. FSIS will also develop compliance guidelines that retailers can use to meet FSIS trace back and trace forward activities, and additional guidance for investigators focused on activities at the retail level.

As mandated by the FSMA, FDA will consider information gathered through pilot tests of approaches to effective product tracing in other food categories, work with the food industry to foster innovative

---

1. To illustrate, FSIS's Office of Public Health Science investigated 16 cases of foodborne illness implicating raw ground beef products manufactured at retail in 2007-2008. Of the 16, only 9 retail operations kept production logs (e.g., grinding logs) sufficient for trace back and trace forward activities. Of the 9, 5 resulted in a recall. (See www.fsis.usda.gov/PPT/Recordkeeping_Presentation.ppt).

> **Next Steps:**
> FDA will work with the food industry to foster innovative approaches to improve tracing, and improve its internal systems for tracing food products to their origin.

approaches to improve tracing, and improve its internal systems for tracing food products to their origin.

C. Improved Response

1. Outbreak Response

By all accounts, the government response to recent multistate outbreaks has been effective in swiftly reducing risks and saving lives. Our new systems were put to the test with the recent Listeria outbreak in cantaloupes. Enhanced surveillance, coordinated by CDC, and a rapid, multistate response were critical in controlling the outbreak. Close collaboration between FDA, CDC and the state of Colorado resulted in quick identification and recall of the contaminated cantaloupes of the source of the contaminated cantaloupes, enabling consumers to be advised quickly to avoid the contaminated food, and helping to prevent further exposures, illnesses, and deaths.

Within a week of FDA issuing a press release announcing the single source of contaminated cantaloupes and that the cantaloupes were recalled, FDA had a multi-disciplinary team on the ground conducting an environmental assessment to better understand how the contamination occurred. Updates on the recall and sub-recalls are posted on FDA's website to ensure consumer awareness.

We continue to dedicate resources and expertise to learn all that we can from these outbreaks, in order to identify risks in advance of future outbreaks. FDA evaluates information, including environmental and product samples used to determine the root-cause of how whole cantaloupe became contaminated

> **Next Steps:**
> The FSIS will propose a rule to enhance our ability to identify outbreaks associated with ground beef from retail stores.

with Listeria. It is clear that we have already realized positive gains from our investment to develop an improved system. For instance, the funding we provided to the state of Colorado to improve surveillance for foodborne illnesses through its participation in the FoodNet active surveillance system, a program sponsored by CDC, FDA, and USDA was instrumental in enabling officials in Colorado to quickly recognize the outbreak of listeriosis cases and conduct interviews to help identify the most likely food associated with the illnesses.

FDA has also recruited a Chief Medical Office/Director of Outbreaks, who will lead a new Coordinated Outbreak Response and Evaluation (CORE) Network within FDA to ensure rapid and effective emergency response and more systematic follow up investigations, in collaboration with CDC and other agencies. Future prevention efforts will be created based on lessons from past outbreak experiences. CDC will continue to evaluate the best methods in FoodCORE Sentinel Sites and will promote best practices among all local and state health departments.

> **Next Steps:**
>
> Using sophisticated data collection and analysis, FSIS will better identify food safety risks before they reach consumers.

2. Data Analysis

In April 2011, FSIS launched the Public Health Information System (PHIS) to help respond more rapidly to current and potential food safety threats. PHIS, which will strengthen FSIS detection and response to foodborne hazards, will be a flexible, user-friendly, and web-based application that replaces many of FSIS' legacy systems, such as Performance Based Inspection System (PBIS) and the Automated Import Information System (AIIS), automates paper-based business processes, and can be modified to accommodate changing needs. PHIS uses a systems approach to food safety. Through its predictive analytics component, PHIS will integrate FSIS' data streams. This function will support a data-driven approach to FSIS inspection, auditing, and scheduling and result in a comprehensive, timely, and reliable data-driven inspection system.

Once fully implemented, PHIS will revolutionize the agency's ability to utilize data in real time to inform all aspects of its domestic inspection, import inspection, and export activities.

This system will make the Agency and its employees more accountable, and allow FSIS to collect more information about the U.S. domestic and international food safety systems, which produce FSIS-regulated products. Using multiple data sources, PHIS will allow analysts to identify trends that will provide the agency with the capability to adjust domestic and import inspection and sampling. As a result, FSIS will be in a position to better identify food safety risks and detect problems before they reach consumers and result in outbreaks and recalls. PHIS will enable alerts for imported product to be triggered by real time data monitoring and will automate FSIS' risk-based approach to foreign country audits and re-inspection. In addition, work will continue under the Data Analysis and Integration Group (DAIG) at FSIS to coordinate the agency's data collection, analysis, and integration activities across all program areas. Also, the FSIS, FDA and CDC have established the Interagency Food Safety Analytics Collaboration (IFSAC) group to develop and share analytical methods, common terminology, and standards of practice. The IFSAC will address key issues such as foodborne illness attribution.

D. Consumer Education

Consumers play a key role in the farm-to-table approach to food safety. They are the last step where food can be contaminated to a level that could cause harm and where proper handling can minimize the risk of harm. Consumer education will therefore continue to be an important part of prevention, as well as the target for information during a food recall or outbreak to identify and prevent use of products that should not be consumed. The FSWG agencies will focus on three areas for improving consumer education:

- elevating interagency and community-based partnerships for food safety education;
- expanding the science base and reach of consumer education; and
- strengthening risk communication related to foodborne outbreaks and recalls.

E. Partnerships

A central element of the vision laid out by the FSMA is that no one agency, level of government or private sector initiative can succeed in meeting today's food safety challenges alone—collaborative action and effective partnerships are vital. Food safety presents many challenges for the entire food system, public and private, and from farm-to-table. Meeting the challenges across organizational lines within government and between government and the private sector is the vision of the FSWG, and the members of the FSWG are committed to fulfilling it.

Many ongoing partnership efforts are outlined in this report. Future efforts will involve the many instances in which FSMA mandates inter-agency collaboration and coordination among federal agencies on such topics as produce safety, preventive controls in food facilities, intentional adulteration standards, technical assistance for small growers and facility operators, and improving surveillance of foodborne illness.

The partnership efforts will also focus heavily on strengthening the capacity of state and local agencies and integrating federal, state and local efforts for a more effective and efficient food safety system, as well as collaborating with foreign governments of import safety.

Finally, government must continue to partner with the food industry and consumers to ensure food safety. Industry bears the primary burden and responsibility to produce safe food, and has vast experience and expertise in doing so. Consumers are also critical partners in the food safety system and in ensuring better outcomes. To be successful, government must further enlist the effort, expertise and perspectives of all stakeholders through systematic outreach and active listening. The FSWG and its members are committed to fostering and maintaining that partnership to sustain and enhance our current system, and continue to provide one of the safest food supplies in the world.

www.ingramcontent.com/pod-product-compliance
Lightning Source LLC
Chambersburg PA
CBHW081818170526
45167CB00008B/3455